ISBN 978-1-4234-7061-8

HAL•LEONARD®
CORPORATION

7777 W. BLUEMOUND RD. P.O. BOX 13819 MILWAUKEE, WI 53213

In Australia Contact:
Hal Leonard Australia Pty. Ltd.
4 Lentara Court
Cheltenham, Victoria, 3192 Australia
Email: ausadmin@halleonard.com.au

edward

twilight

bella

twilight

james

twilight

WHO ARE THEY?

Composed by
CARTER BURWELL

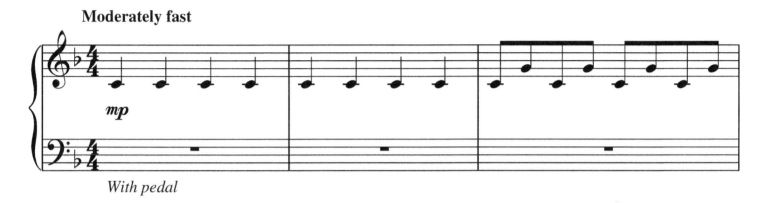

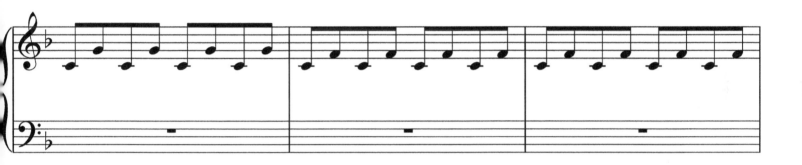

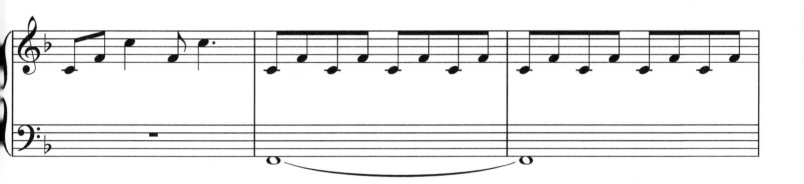

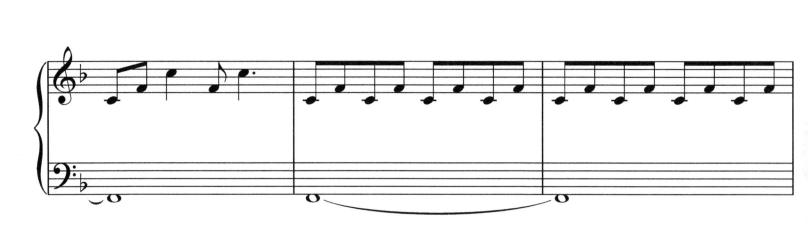

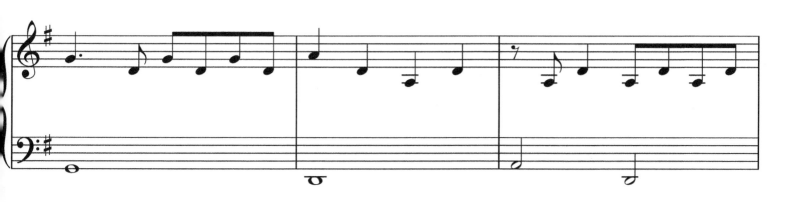

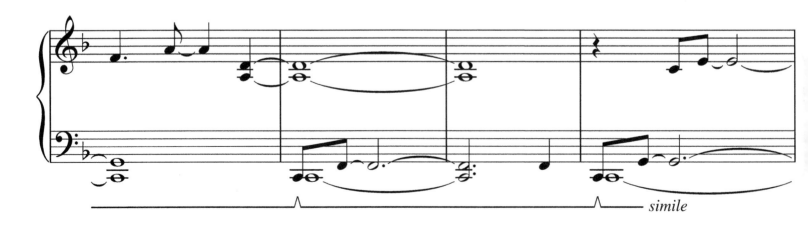

simile

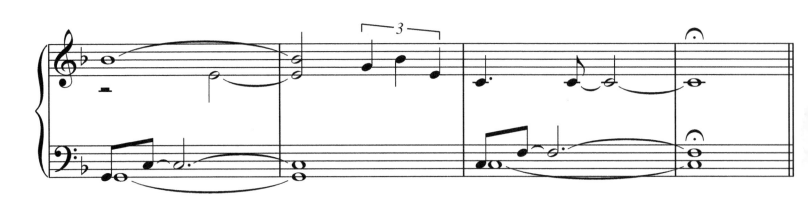

Slightly slower

PHASCINATION PHASE

Composed by
CARTER BURWELL

Moderately slow, in 2

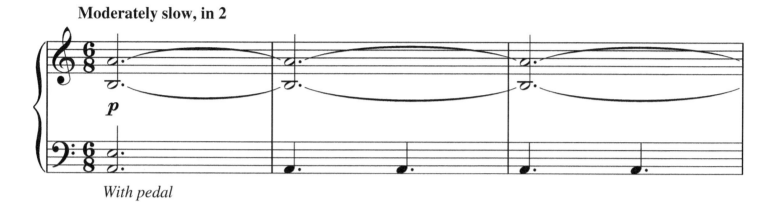

With pedal

I DREAMT OF EDWARD

Composed by
CARTER BURWELL

DINNER WITH HIS FAMILY

Composed by
CARTER BURWELL

THE LION FELL IN LOVE WITH THE LAMB

Composed by
CARTER BURWELL

Moderately slow, in 2

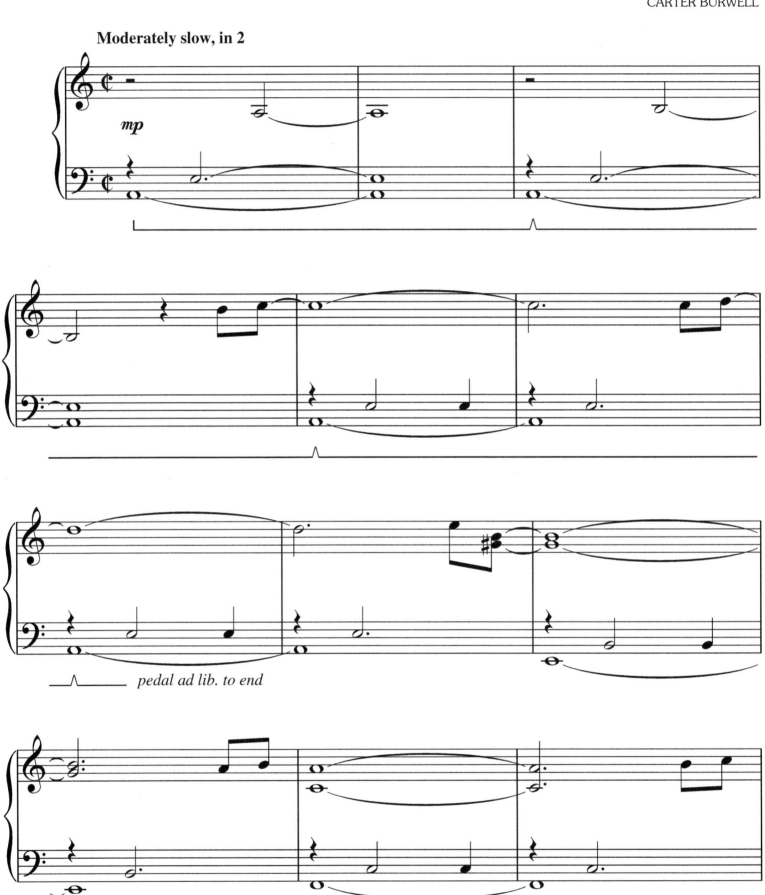

pedal ad lib. to end

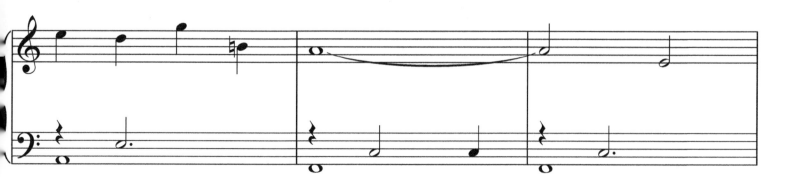

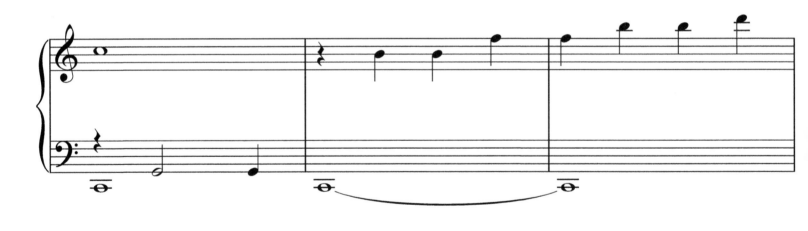

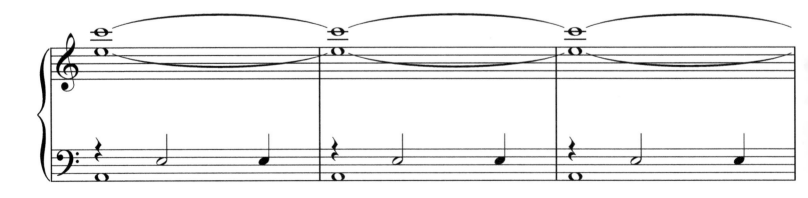

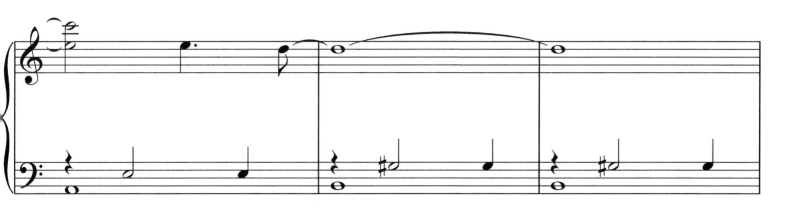

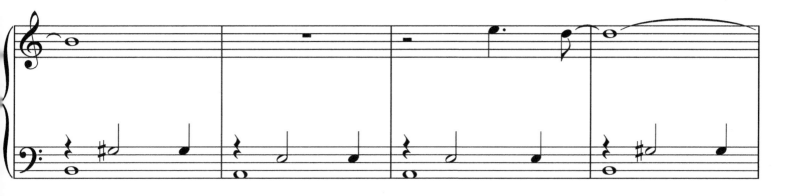

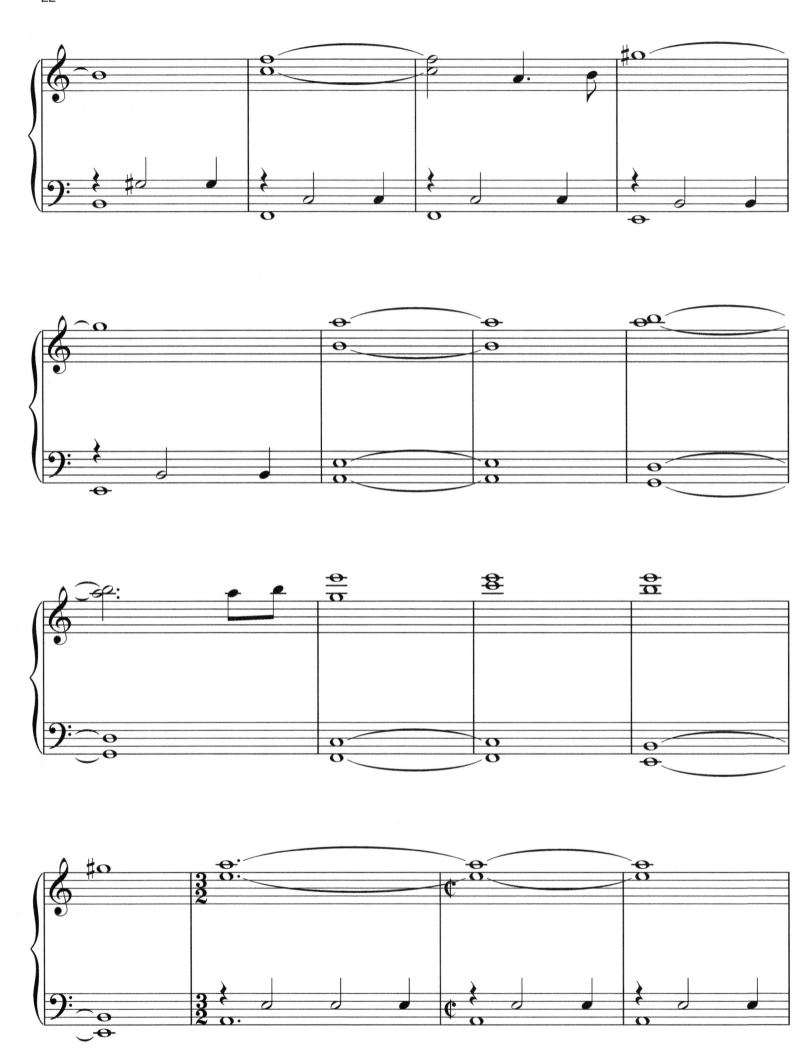

I WOULD BE THE MEAL

Composed by
CARTER BURWELL

Moderately

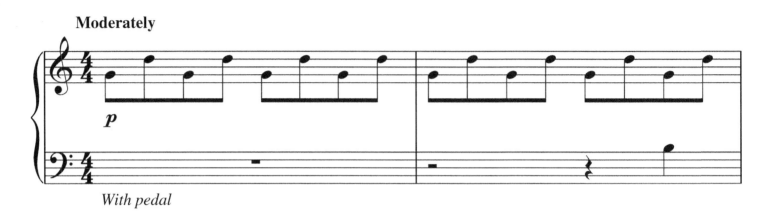

With pedal

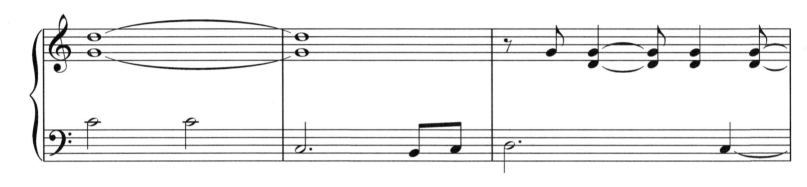

BELLA'S LULLABY

Composed by
CARTER BURWELL

Moderately

mp

With pedal

p

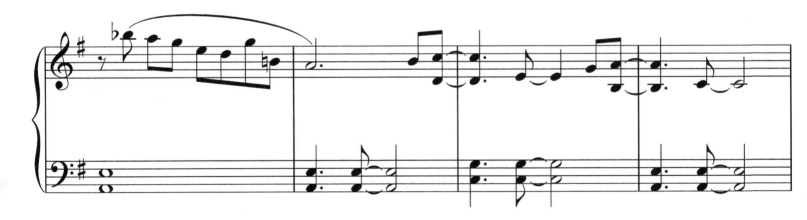

STUCK HERE LIKE MOM

Composed by
CARTER BURWELL

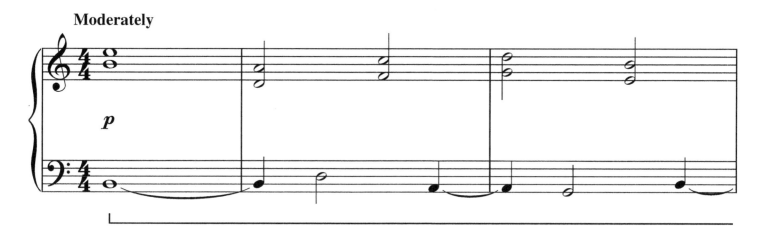

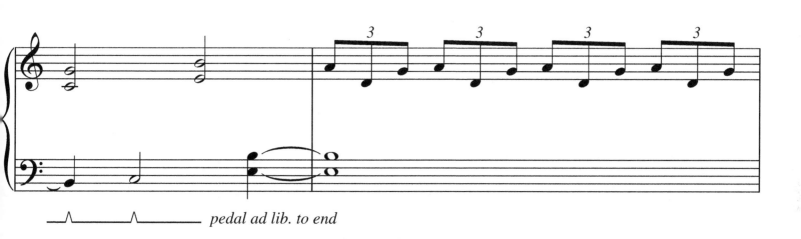

pedal ad lib. to end

TRACKING

Composed by
CARTER BURWELL

Slowly, in 2

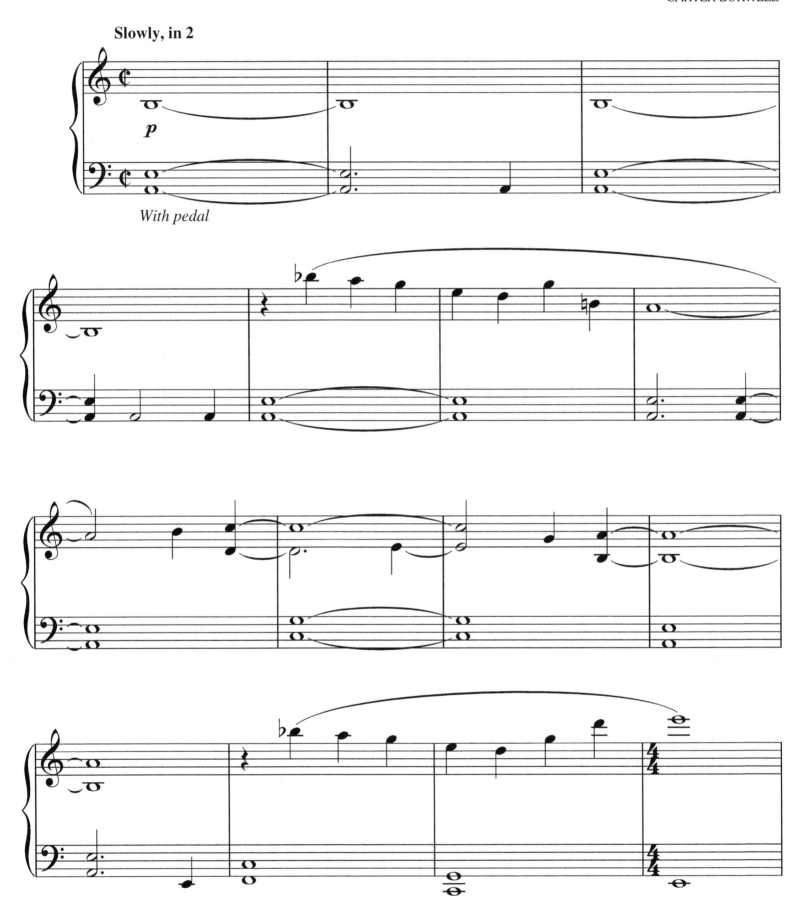

With pedal

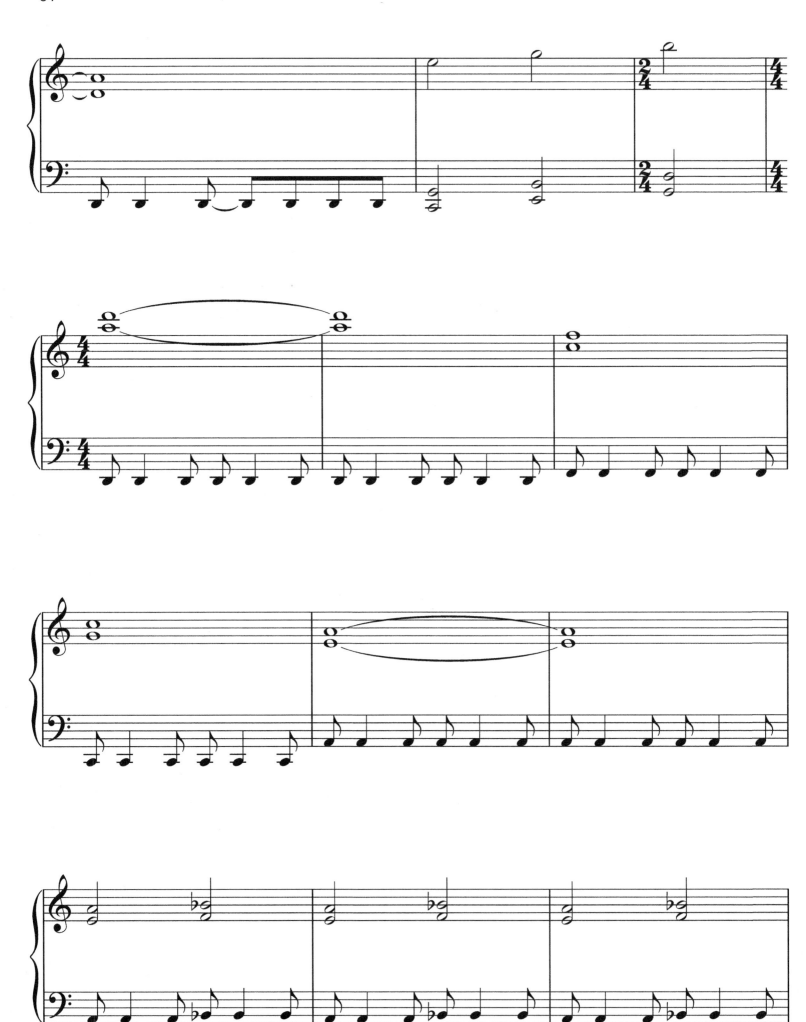

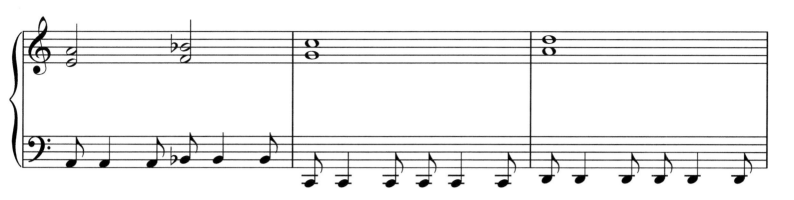

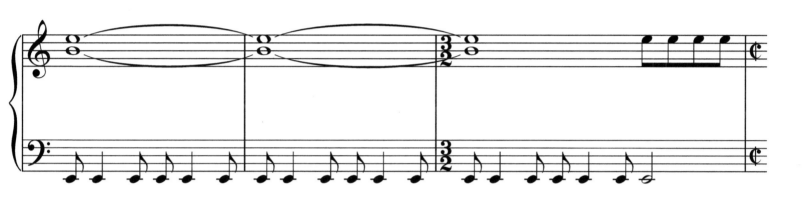

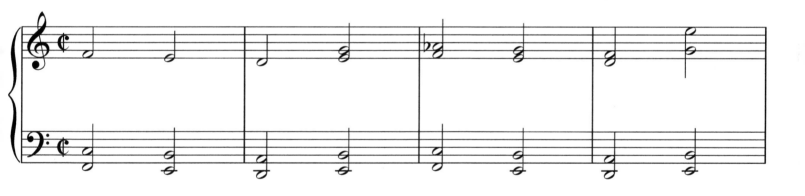

IN PLACE OF SOMEONE YOU LOVE

Composed by
CARTER BURWELL

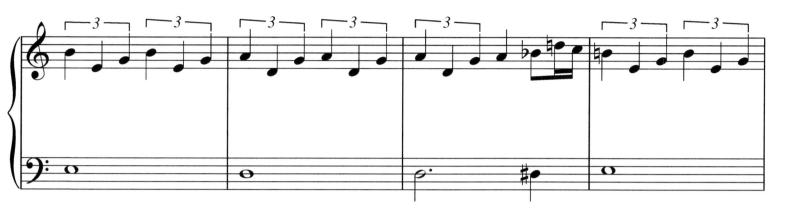

EDWARD AT HER BED

Composed by
CARTER BURWELL